SCREAM
INTO MY
MOUTH
AS A
WATERFALL

SCREAM
INTO MY
MOUTH
AS A
WATERFALL

poems & prose

C. Aloysius Mariotti

Rhythm & Bones Press
Trauma-turned-Art

Rhythm & Bones Press
Birdsboro, Pennsylvania

Scream into my Mouth as a Waterfall
© 2020 C. Aloysius Mariotti
© 2020 Rhythm & Bones Press

Interior Design: Tianna G. Hansen, Rhythm & Bones Press
Cover Art: Mathew Yates
Illustrations by: Mathew Yates, Stuart Buck
ISBN: 978-1-952050-00-8
First Edition March 2020

www.rhythmnbone.com/c-aloysius-mariotti

∞

Content Warning: Much of these pieces involve the darker side of human nature and deal with trauma including child abuse, infanticide, violence involving sexual assault, drug abuse, among others. Please take care while reading.

Advance praise for *Scream into my Mouth as a Waterfall*

∞

"In *Scream into my Mouth as a Waterfall,* C. Aloysius Mariotti takes us 'raw and exposed' through an American dreamscape where 'the very nature of life [is] demolished ready for rebirth'. In this dazzling collection, linear time, hierarchies and identities collapse and the reader is left alone at the haunting edgelands of the desert, the gateway to infinity. Fantastical, uncanny illustrations by Mathew Yates and Stuart Buck compliment Mariotti's utterly authentic poetic voices. One of the poetry collections of the year."

— Matthew M.C. Smith, poet and editor of Black Bough Poetry

"What amazes me most about C. Aloysius Mariotti's new book, *Scream into My Mouth as a Waterfall,* is how seamlessly the pieces fit together to forge a portrait of real courage. Poem by poem, these fractals combine into an architecture of love, fear, power, dread, and, best of all, raw feeling. There's the purity of a young boy riding his bike down the street, the release of a son resting his tired feet in a river, the promise of a first kiss, and beautiful burst of sky glowing here. There is also the black hole of loss, the tightening walls of death lurking in these shadows. Nothing about this book ducks life's punch. Just as nothing about this poet shuns life's embrace. Every page of *Scream into My Mouth as a Waterfall* knows full well you have to lean into one to smile in the glow of the other."

— Jack B. Bedell, Poet Laureate, State of Louisiana, 2017-2019, author of *No Brother, This Storm*

"C. Aloysius Mariotti's *Scream into my Mouth as a Waterfall* explores grief and love—birth and death; what it means to be everything and nothing. With subtlety and precision, Mariotti effortlessly captures what it means to be human with exquisite use of form, language, and tension. This collection's intertwining of written and visual art characterizes every presence and makes us feel the physical experience of each piece's speaker. This debut collection was breathed into life with color, sound, and intense care."

— Savannah Slone, author of *An Exhalation of Dead Things* and *Hearing the Underwater*

"The interplay of fact and myth is so beautifully woven throughout this first book effort by C. Aloysius Mariotti; the personal and surreal collide and caress. This whole book delights as much as it dizzies in its examination of life and landscape from mysterious angles. As the title poem says of its primary character, this body of work, too, will 'haunt from haunt to haunt.'"

— K. Weber, author of *THIS ASSEMBLY*

"*Scream into my Mouth as a Waterfall* is a captivating read from beginning to end. It's an existential thrill ride through the seismic highs and unrelenting lows of the human condition, a collection of works that stick with you long after the page has turned. These words are visions that you'll see behind closed eyelids, and feel entwined into your own personal experiences."

— Chip McCabe, author of *666 Days of Metal*

"Mariotti's debut collection is full of comets and rain and night sky and pears and bones and graveyards for those bones to lay. And magic. Of course, magic. Declaring, 'but we are creatures,' from the onset, Mariotti wants to remind you of our smallness, our humanness, our animalness. That we all have a beginning and an expiration date, how actions have lasting consequences regardless of our indifference, of the summersaults our memory performs—fragments, like lost tiny vertebrae, these pieces of fragile bone when combined create a powerful structure. ... What makes this work shine is the poet's commitment to not thinking himself infallible, admitting we must take one day at a time. At times conversational and at others prophetic, *Scream into my Mouth as a Waterfall* feels like sitting across from a stranger at a bar overhearing pieces of a story, and finding yourself not wanting to get up and leave until the puzzle is finished. What makes these truths universal is that even if the story is not about us, we can find some piece of us in it. That's what great writing does, and this is fantastic writing."

— Keegan Lester, author of
this shouldn't be beautiful but it was and it was all i had so i drew it

contents

∞

This book is dedicated to all the gorgeous misfits.
Never stop being.

♡

∞

"The true profession of man is to find his way to himself."

— Hermann Hesse

"We look at the world once, in childhood. The rest is memory."

— Louise Glück

"We are torn between nostalgia for the familiar and an urge for the foreign and strange. As often as not, we are homesick most for the places we have never known."

— Carson McCullers

"It is by no means an irrational fancy that, in a future existence, we shall look upon what we think our present existence, as a dream."

— Edgar Allan Poe

"Being with you and not being with you is the only way I have to measure time."

— Jorge Luis Borges

"Wilderness of mirrors
So easy to deceive
My precious sense of rightness
Is sometimes so naive
So that which I imagine
Is that which I believe."

— Neil Peart

∞

the pendulum swings a strange loop

allow me to start by saying I am afraid of death—that of a lover, or a friend, or a kinsman, or a pet, or a stranger, or my own. we are all creatures that breathe and run and love and laugh and fuck and feed; but we are creatures who will one day burden the cold dirt to intrude our lungs, and paralyze our limbs, and dampen our hearts, and silence our bellies.

we all die, my children.

saint de los milagros

I'm a shape shifter, man—a common *nagual*.

when the moon opens in the mexican sky, I cross over canals to eat your heart—I scrabble your skin and open wounds that pound hard for release into new inner orbits. how can you circle a sun you cannot see? I bring it to you, friend. I lay it in your palm for you to learn to watch without burning your eyes. I bring you to where you never were, down sharp corridors to swallow the great wonder of life and death.

but I'm just a man in the dry daytime desert. I have a wife and child and struggles. I have no money and a mother with cancer. I have pain in my heart that pulses when I drop my feet into the hot river behind my home, and the prattle of water over the large stones floods my hope for escape, my throbbing heart further squeezed so it becomes lead in the liquid below me.

I stay until nighttime, when I move with haste toward the bloodletting. I pounce on you as if it were me—I give to you what I cannot give to myself,

that beautiful escape to spots beyond this consciousness, to a chance to see light beyond the curve and spiral.

I wondered about love for a moment

about the shape of it, the points and curves of something that tucked itself into us as a concept. love is like this neighborhood we are in—all the different houses appear tangible, as concrete structures of brick-and-mortar. but the inside of each shines with specific intensity

as the warmth of photos and knick-knacks to one equals the beauty of saltillo tile and orange-painted bedroom walls to another. we imagine what pleases us, feel the heartbeats of our perfect houses

whether along the shoreline or along a mountain road, or atop the cool midnight grass of a public park—

love is ours.

in vertigo

On the other side of the room is a worn wooden tabletop strewn with fabric and photographs from a perfect world, so my head tries to sew together mosaics from then to now:

There's a young boy on a slide in a tree-littered park. There's a young boy riding a bicycle on a rain-soaked sidewalk. There's a young boy blowing out candles on a frosty-dark chocolate cake. There's a young boy holding hands with his dad on an orange bench.

There's a letter you sent me, torn from a manila envelope, that reads: *thought you'd like to have these back?*

And I wish I had a candle that smells like the beach—sand, gushing water, suntan lotion, vacationers from Pennsylvania, seagull feathers, ice cream, and french fries, and a particular day in early summertime many years ago, when I kissed a girl named Samira behind the public showers—all mixed together with wax and wick. I had a dog who would chase me in the backyard and pummel me with his large soft tongue all over my face. Often, we would walk through the cemetery after school to chase birds and lay ourselves on the warm grass between gravestones to look at the sky. The sun crossed above us motionless, like our sleeping bone-neighbors; a static ataraxy, the sweet spot of abundant tranquility for us two. But despite our closeness, he was never allowed to the beach because of currents and seaweed and a lack of interest in doggie-paddles or floaties. Though he was well-behaved around girls and would seek them out for scratches and feet to sit upon. He'd have liked Samira. And the seagulls, and the ice cream, and the french fries, too.
  His name was Samson.

I remember rambling through the schoolyard at midnight to steal a kiss from Samantha while her friends rooted on from the drinking fountain near the cafeteria because her parents wouldn't allow boys to the slumber party, and it was romantic for them to climb down the fence all secretive-like for a sneak with a boy. To kiss her over and over I soothed in my heart, my Samantha, my first kiss, my fleeting beauty that moved to San Mateo five days later.

∞

Light falls from the sky to possess the leaning curves outside the shadows. Maple soaks into the earth below, tangled roots and lush meadow. Chocolate hides under my pillow so the room smells like childhood vacations to the

5

countryside near old brick buildings and soda fountains. Your kisses remain on my mouth and taste like plums and licorice and long weekends at the shore, and how I miss those trips, and how I miss my youth.

I met her in a corner bar on Main Street, she in plaid skirt and Doc Martens. I'm Lorelei, she said. And for the night it was her name in my mouth instead of yours:

O a shot and a whiskey and a stout and O a shot and a whiskey and a stout and O a nudge in the front seat in the parking lot and O a rub on the hip and sighs fogging the glass and O a push inside and clutches and moans and slippery and O a kiss farewell and O a kiss farewell and adieu and goodbye and O a kiss and oh! oh! oh!

I stand in the Garden of Forking Paths every time I close my eyes. And when I open them, the whole bloody thing is ablaze! The pendulum swings a strange loop as we move from birth to death to birth and so forth, so we can come to understand why we move at all. The crush and merge into the *rubedo*—we become the Completeness.

∞

Upon your bosom I laid my head, my love. I heard the pulse of life in resonant undulations. They beat my mistakes because my mistakes became yours to bear as our hearts entwined like two vines growing together needing the same nourishment, sprawling to touch boundaries they cannot inhabit separately.

Each misstep tripped us to learn again to climb with wiser footing, so we may find atonement in those blurry moments. To be a pick in the ice, to chisel away the cold stars in the sky that shone upon crooked monstrous paths so that we learned to give reason to the weight of our own compass.

We laid next to each other smelling of beaches, and of the years that existed not forthwith but pocketed out there, just waiting for us.

And I am dizzy from existence.

desert diptych

the desert was my home

the sun that is torrid
scorch-dark
desolate draggletailed landscape
burning sand
ululates
a split in the sky.

faraway stars eat time

star-death spreads through infinite galaxies,
dashing toward planets not yet born—drifts
of fury and awe travelled.

a saguaro stands high, beckoning
suns in the night-sky—their expiry
as incandescent explosions:

celestial parade of dead lovers—
pinholes outside stygian desert edges.

modern pip, fragmented

I.

the circle stopped spinning at 7:03 am
when I first slid into the world
bald and tiny and trembling
and reaching to go back.

my mother held me close to her breast
she kissed my fevered forehead and named me
philip pirrip. my bitty hands were curled
clutching for her long brown hair
and with a singular murmur
I intimated to the world that I was here
yeah—I was here indeed. because what choice had I?

if I could quote latin then, I'd have entered the world
a scholar, a philosopher, a story they'd all remember:

annus mirabilis—hic puer est stultissimus omnium!

of course, I knew no language
but that of moans and sobs. and why not?
it's the language of lovers and the youth.

because the wonder years of an american youth begin when we stop breathing
that symbiotic life of cramped home and they end when we stop to understand
those moments that led us to where we are.

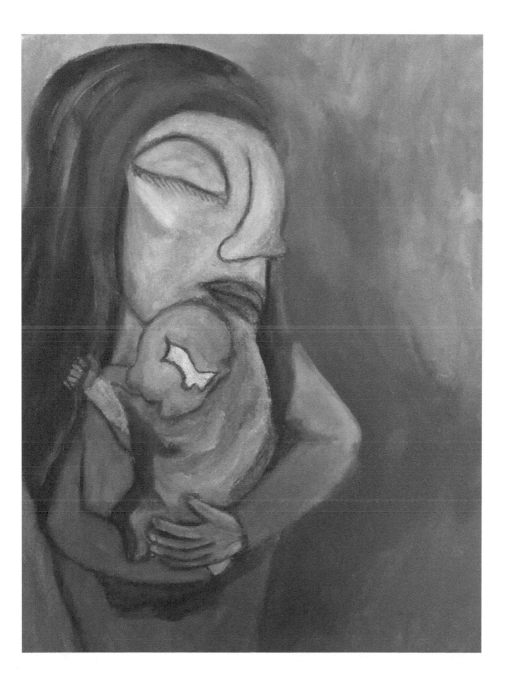

II.

I'd watch her aglow beneath phoenician moons
on countless nights
as she danced between gravestones to clutch god
from skin embraces, atop tombs of the sexless dead.

rum in her belly rum on her lips bruise on her hips
she was the girl after whom to
      sleep sleep sleep
and bathe in the river lethe
so I won't remember what she will
those punches and pounds
        and moans O the moans
to be treated unlike the neighbor girl
with the pretty picket fence and geraniums on the porch
and pigtails and corduroy.

we met and held hands past the bus stop
we rambled on to that spot as teenagers
to that empty lot, to kiss and profess
      mad young love
until I waited and waited for her to come to me again.

estella
she moved like a comet
her traces left in that empty lot
that became a damn graveyard
of bones and memories.

III.

he thought she tasted like rain and pears and
a thousand past lovers. they slid into his mouth
to unravel the invincible days
now whirling in space and memory, the tatterings of nights
in empty parks and bathroom stalls
the yellowed snapshots of moonlit howlings wrapped in earth
of roiled knees and bruised woman-sheath
of spoiled prudence and no-way-backs.

he thought she sounded like a whale on the beach
clamoring for the water of her mother's womb
the tight and unharmed spot rejecting ingress
and burden and heartbreak.

and he wondered why she came to him, while she moaned against his ears,
as she shook like a blade of grass
right before the cut.

IV.

but we were good old mates we were—estella and me
two coins in the pocket of the earth.

and I think about that spot where we were
then we weren't
and this one wound up here
as that one wound up there after the scatter
and I linger on the line
that angles toward infinity
distant from our point of singularity.

and though our new towns have the same strip malls and exxon stations and
sad eyes of the streets, the familiarity gets scratched enough to show a scar
unique to the separate faces we put on each morning in the different towns
alike.

and the one we once knew together
before the collapse of the gravity holding us
to our shared living star

is now long ashed and floating
to a faraway halt.

V.

estella would sneak through the cellar door

to lie in the cherry orchard behind her uncle's farmhouse
where she'd stare into myriad opulent stars
and smell delicious purple blossoms,

and bury her tired fingers
into the dirt that tucked her parents
beneath her trembling bones to loathe.

and the short sharp shocks to her heartsick dithers
would be to remember their faces
against the rounded hilltop before the tumbles.

and the push / the crash / the lull / the end.

and screak is the soaking echo
like in the hollow of a cobbled water well
it is the sound and howl

that pushed through the earth and vibrated
at the tips of her curled fingers
as she would reach down to touch her parents once more

beneath the tilted moon.

VI.

what a distant ballet she danced
entangled in the mess of skin and moan through ohio
all blurred to rub past windows darkly moon-hued and fogged
because to stop
                    would be to forgive
                              would be to shudder
                                        would be to die
beneath paler thoughts than hers from the push and carry.

don't go, he mouthed. but her eyes obeyed
only the goodbyes littered down by stars
from towns dull and orange in thick still dusk
and the motionless forgotten
and onward she roved and onward she burned
through the scores of lost
and longer faces.

VII.

moving inside sheets electric
to let it out
and falling into place
with stroke
and undulation
and pausing
to the morning thereafter
behind the bending sun

and collapsing the dark spots
between hello and goodbye.

VIII.

estella spoke
to the salt and the sea
as the machine crushed lilies into floating hearts
and foam and smoke and metal
and mermaids who fell
toward languorous hollows.

and dizzy was the spiral
to enchant the slumbering of purple days
adrift voluminous waves
without song or rum
for the delicate and heartsick shipwrecked
cold from the drowning moonlight
to bathe lost skin in the velvet tomorrows of estella
but curves with shut eyes to tripping beats of time
and again it will start.

IX.

the mission bell rung lonesome
crushing the noiseless winter horizon of the desert
where she used to suck her skins
and smoke her bones
while chewing datura seeds
to collapse beneath large saguaros
and rave at the chilling moon.

what pauses she overlooked
like thin breath fogging glass
leaving markers but small proof of the slips
and swallows and dark sand
in the corners of her chapped mouth.

those nights when crooked earth was mattress
and scuffed legs eased penetrations
none of which she would cull as unforced
but often were sought from the break of
cold mornings in the suburbs.

but she seemed to always furl toward the sloping of low horizon
saying pull me under pull me under
break me asunder.

X.

the drunk recrudesced from still quiescence
                naked
and feeling a bit tawdry and lost
from disconnect of the star
in gloaming to the east.

I sipped and stretched dirty fingers and indecorous tongue
toward the dullard shines
that only traced the spaces near me
floating opposite my mania
like an ocean too shallow to drown.

but then I stumbled over a seashell
that was lovely, delicate, one of a kind.

and I wondered about what I would learn if I pressed my muddled ears against
its heart. so I slept on the beach to dream of stars rising again in the sober east
beneath a windless morning that was like every other.

XI.

       that empty lot.
I'd pass it like a sozzled russian poet
stumbling, screaming how I saw beauty
in the hash of stone & metal & broken rubble

       raw and exposed
the very nature of life demolished
ready for rebirth.

and I hoped to capture the transition
or I hoped to capture the dirge it hummed
       of life no longer astir.

because what wonder it held to others
was the wonder it held to me as I passed it
       that empty lot.

backdrifting

because the ghost of the divorce vociferates
      I squeeze at my ears and wait for the shift
            into the dream-sepulcher of goodbyes—

I know this place, verdant meadow swallowed on each side by fat rolling green hills. but I cannot reach them no matter how fast or far I walk. so I lay myself in the grass and stare at dancing clouds as they transfer forms into more familiar creations.

the one farthest east looks like my childhood home in greensburg, with red bricks and a sticker of a fireman's silhouette holding an axe on the upstairs bedroom window. the one in the north resembles the snowman I built with my brother in our grandparents' yard when I was in kindergarten, even having the coal we used for his left eye. but where is his right eye? and I don't remember his face frowning; or did it?

and the one in the south turns into a blue pickup truck stuffed with picture books and clothes and bicycles—no, now it's distorting into a face as the sky changes to a howling darkness with ferocious wind and sounds are a dissonance of fast voices and wails and the cloud-face grows pointed teeth that almost touch me while I'm motionless / paralyzed I can only shut my eyes so hard that blood pours down my skin.

then all wind and sounds cease.

when I open my eyes I'm in an empty playground at lehi elementary. I ramble to the swings. I want to fly but my legs stick in the ground like drums of lead—
            do you want me to push?
it's my father, standing behind me with a baseball glove on his left hand. I tell him yes, and so he pushes. as I gain speed and rise higher I can see beyond the trees in front of me. in the dark distance is a house with a chimney blowing smoke that arranges upward into a heart.

as I reach the downswing, I feel my father's hand on my back. just as he pushes off, he says something to me—
            goodbye, son.

∞

I drove down jasmine street to see the house I grew up in. coming home from college, it seemed like all my former haunts changed—baseball fields became apartments; dairy queen became a sonic burger; tri-city mall became a vacant building surrounded by chain-link fence. and my old house became home to a new bright-eyed suburban family of two parents and 1.14 children.

and it looked so small, there. plants wrapped around the front porch, and the basketball hoop attached to the roof was gone. our gravel yard and cactus garden turned into abundant green and waterfall. it was like looking into a friend's face after he returned from an existential sabbatical—new lines, new blushes, almost now a damn stranger.

how much living I did in that three-bedroom house! the holidays and sleepovers, the late-night movies, the dinners, the breakdowns, the make-ups, the make-outs, the discovery of guns n' roses—christ, the first time I masturbated was in that house.

but the landscape changes. like how continents were once joined and time pushed them apart, so is our youth—our memories get scattered across our brains, and hearts, some even go forgotten into the depths. and as new ones are made by new people, we try to recover our own.

∞

those things that stick alone in memory sometimes glue against another stranger image from our past to form an unlikely synchronicity as pure and stark as anything in a dali dream.

whenever I hear *Man in the Mirror* I taste the strong soapy chlorinated water of the carson junior high swimming pool. but why?

maybe I was held underneath during 8th grade gym class as a prank and the foul tasting broth shot into my mouth and I swallowed it like gnats swarmed in a hot summer park and my eyes burned as I looked for a faraway out and I came to the surface to cough ferociously to dry my lungs and all the other boys laughed and I sat hunched and dull through my afternoon classes then shuffled my shoes along the sidewalk from the bus stop to home then lurched onto my bed and turned on the radio and *Man in the Mirror* played as I thought about what happened earlier.

or, neither song nor moment rode the same buzzing end of my wires as I lived that last spring in my home before the separation of mother and father and middle bedroom on jasmine street—but the fragments blurred into a marvelous mess like molasses to fatten the need to understand why this happens to that.

∞

mister morrow, they said

time rubs against the insides of your skull,
and fast
       —tom, they said—
       you can't outrun yourself.

because moments push that inerasable crush from then to now to when, and we sit tired of the loop that moves fast with every scent and scene paralyzing us to the moments of the push.

pithy, these clicks in the rolling wheel that smash too soon the lovely touches and sounds of don't-forgets, yes? but we blur to barely remember and thus puzzle the dizzy dids and did-we-dids that make up our past.

though to look forward—will we walk because of where we have been? does our reflection show edges we think we can smooth by tracing the cuts and blood we left in the wake of our tuition?

what do we learn? *what can we learn from learning what we learn?*

oh mister morrow! you're naked against the curves of the ho-hum!
       tom tom tom   this is the spot!
reach into the unknown—scrunch together the corners

so they may kiss each other
beneath uncommon stars
and maddened wonders

you've yet to dally toward, and tease, and taste.

panikos the sailor

a panic beneath the lunar sea—this is the cycle of my disorder.

I crouch to peer at the night sky, to see the spinning above me as humming aeroplanes seem to connect distant stars that linger on their fixed points. they are diminutive in the darkness like pupils in the eyes of madmen who saunter through despoiled city streets or shrubbery in backyards or the hearts of young stranger girls. as I now lie on the pavement I think of my disease that creeps through my cells and expels out my pores and then regenerates in my brain and makes me dizzy and nervous and frightened and somewhat near the thought that I am dying all over again and again and again while the noises around me surge and throb and the images around me expand and shake so that I feel smothered and unable to regain control until twenty minutes can pass and the pill takes hold but in the meantime I am sweating and buzzing and whirring and racing and pounding and yelping and cognizant that these will pass but not until they pass, much like a song with a lovely chorus that is interrupted by a bridge that changes keys for exactly five measures and undulates in the ears discordantly and frenetic but will eventually return to the sweet refrain of the chorus, the sweet refrain of the chorus, yes it will return to that refrain and all will again be right. I know it is coming but must endure the moments that press my pulse and throttle my tuition and squeeze my sensibility. and I think about Sisyphus and how he would need to push his rock up the peak only to have it fall back down again, how he would tolerate the tribulation of the imperfect deed that would never go away, how he knew what would always happen when he reached near the top, and how he never found a way to push himself into the ground instead.

this is the cycle of my disorder—a panic beneath the lunar sea.

impeachment day

raffish, a brute—and cunning his tongue and hold. with the ice cream, and the comics, and the nintendo.

he would let us ride on his lap in that curtained penthouse, we the latchkeys. he would let us pose for photos while saving the princess, or stabbing the goblin, and we giggled shirtless and loose until twilight edged against the horizon and supper was only doors away.

AND IT'S TO BE OUR TREMENDOUS SECRET!

my mother used to say what a lonely man donald was. his ruffled hair was a picture of the mess beneath it—the charred wiring, the distorted feelings that would gush onto we the latchkeys, who sucked it in, really, the affections of that bachelor who was too keen to make us the champions of epics and pubescent rowdiness, or restlessness, or certain obliviousness.

a boy shouldn't lose his virginity at ten years old while immured in devastating fear on rough orange carpet, his innocence impeached and torn raw. not with the smell of pepperoni pizza burning the walls, nor with the taste of entitled on the mouth of his wolfish captor—the kind of creature he would slay with his fellow latchkeys in arms, but never once could he slay alone.

and maybe none of them could, as secrets die with us in the oblong rot lost beneath gravestones, and memories.

modern adonis

I loiter in the vernal days of youth
where I steep myself on the brow of a sodden tree
where cherry blossoms smother the steamy ground
as cuts of green arouse beneath, where birds and bees
crash in the air to halt in a stare of remembrance
when the low sun soaks the pores of waking creatures
when those in want of love and reason know those days
will always be known as the funereal days of youth.

as I struggle with the somber moods of the earth
with the darker movements around me
I slump. to be without insight
drowning in a tidal pool of my own creation
microcosmic, particular to me alone.

so what that daddy turned to dust
that he powdered the cool soil
          of haunted chambers?
is earth not an enormous sepulcher?
          it matters nothing to me
the pokes and scrapes of synthesized events.

          myrrha was a selfish girl, yet she loved.
          she had cause for her affection—sinuous, in absolute beauty,
          she moved as she loved. and I can't recall the last time
          my father offered a hug to me beyond the steel
          he offered to my mother's swollen belly.

perhaps I rest in the arms of myrrha
          these springtime days
and we both weep, because it feels right.

modern paris

a precise smoothness to the touch
this trophy. my fingertips glide
delicate though delirious
with hunger. her surface is cool.
screams may toss about beneath such
bone and blood. but must I hear them?

her marble face and perfumed skin
snap the only senses that care.
for my trophy girl, I've not much
more to pine. I have tasted the
golden apple and swallowed thick
a prize worth nothing to my heart.

lessons triptych

spinning

a former teacher
said once in softer
tone, only to me,
someone will come who is always better.

and still I spin
an imperfect circle
in chase of my vanishing tail.

burning

I ponder all my moments lost
the happy times they spurned
I hearken back to bridges crossed
or rather those that burned.

simplicitas

to pen a poem in latin
would be my heart's delight
but I know not latin now
as I write beneath this light.

so I'll pen this poem in english
my exquisite native tongue
even though 'tis simple
and could leave my work unsung.

lost american gospel of vincent de paul

on an old street in the city, beggars with angular outstretched fingers are
shivering somewhere near east 14th avenue below canopies among the smell of
heated coffee and hot dogs and pretzels
and their wet eyes mirrored off storefront windows
          like dying oceans
as they were turned away before entering
blemished   beaten from the reject of a fellow man
          is there no incorrupt heart willing to favor, they thought?
          do all these passing feet move without charity, they hollered!

and a girl came
streaks like melted coal beneath her eyes
sable-hued hair knotted and disarrayed
in the winter's early moonlight   she howled with each step

and a boy clutched
her denim skirt as she passed him
when she looked down at him
wrapped in a dirty yellow blanket for warmth
          he cut her with his stare   his look of life.

he knew the misfortune of another's stumbles
the sense that she was in a worse place
          at that very moment   than he was

and so he offered his pittance of collection to her. he aimed her toward
the vendor, where she ordered a coffee and a bite

and she came back to the wall
to slink down next to him   to share both with him.

scream into my mouth as a waterfall

I remember watching her live as if a ghost in a churchyard, drifting along pale and quiet, to haunt from haunt to haunt.

I reflect on my own face in the ruddy pub mirror that has me an ocean apart from her delicious face, her slightly tilted neck, the camber of her hip, her tiny arching feet, as she'd lay herself in a curl on the checkered sofa.

my jaw looks like dying grass. whiskers are dull and brown, pointing away from the sun in this dark english town. lips are eclipsed over from stains of too many oatmeal stouts and unfiltered cigarettes. eyes like dim dual moons too low in the grey sky, hoping upward to grow large like multi-colored bulbs in the spring.

she asked if I could stay.

but how could I hold a hand that held a small head beneath the water? a shaking hand too young itself to feed milk and peas over heroin and madness? whose blame sinks more into the earth: that of the addict or the absent?

she'd move about the city barefoot and lusting for ways to drink waterfalls and leap canyons and kiss the stars. then she'd fever and shake and sob until the south pole could hear her, as if she was proserpina trying to punch out of the heart of pluto and her spot in eternity.

all I could do was steal away.

I wouldn't be there to see that little pine box lowered down to escape the hysterical demon lunging for fixes and a solitary euphoria. and me, just as careless, a vanished vapor thinning beyond his toys and crib and fingers and heartbeat and blue eyes,

crystal blue like the water that suffocated him.

june 14, 2005

Because Lorelei had nowhere to go.

Bed sheets were draped atop warped linoleum flooring while running scalding water in the claw-foot, as she began to unravel a rusted wire-hanger.

And here come the Innovators!—rubbed against desperation brings a disguise for madness as she baptized the sharpest end into the water and moaned
not like him, not like them.

And slumping with her back against the tub she wore down the nerve with indelible precision and sobs, impelled to aim her future's curve toward a space wholly separate from the line she thought it would travel—she thought she was moving oceans, she hoped she was coloring the strange sky luscious and large and inimitable.

And up drug the skirt, and down the burgundy cotton, knees at first touching before creeping apart. Her raw taut thighs were pale, so the myriad bruises looked like crushed plums on a sidewalk.

Then came the moment of insertion.

And her thoughts were of dirty mattresses in darker rooms, of punches and ropes and cocaines and madnesses swept beneath haunting moons, moments she moseyed to erase with an abysmal jabbing.

And then a sudden ringing—it was like a bell in a cave bouncing about edgeless and thick and forever. Her eyes crushed together, and she felt moisture flow to places not meant to touch tears; and then came her recorded voice from the next room, imploring
... I can't come now, to reach me you must leave a message....

And then she heard—he was dead, he was gone, he was no more—the monster was slayed.

And she shook, Lorelei did, her body an earthquake beneath the buzzing orange and blue overhead light. She threw aside the wet hanger and bellowed with hysterical ferocity—she rubbed her swollen belly and kissed the air!

It's going to be different now. It's going to be safe now. We'll touch the sun together now.

32

may 10, 1981

— a microplay

A Man and Woman glide slowly on a porch-swing while sounds in the Pennsylvania woods are of natural uneasiness—throbbing chirps and chops of buzzing crickets; deep / sour / mournful moans of creek-toads; maddening swoons and howls of dogs, or wolves, or monsters. She is covered to her shoulders in a wool blanket. His eyes direct themselves to an owl on a branch of an oak tree in the front yard.

MAN: I wonder what goes through their minds?

She thinks for a moment, digresses.

WOMAN: We never should've cut down that tree.
MAN: Yes—but then, my darling, where would you swing every night?
WOMAN: We were very selfish. It should still be standing there, next to its lover.
MAN: But—it was a dying tree.

He reaches over and cradles her left hand between his two.

WOMAN: And here I am—myself dying. With too little time to give back.

She traces the fingertips of her right hand back and forth across the swing's armrest.

She closes her eyes as he sits quietly, his own eyes and mind fixed in thought. He leans over to kiss her on the forehead, rises, and goes through the front screen door.

Sounds of commotion push through the darkness from inside the house. He returns to the porch while holding a few items in his arms. He sits and gently pulls the blanket from her body. She is in a thin nightgown, which he slips off of her delicately, over her head. She gives no resistance. He then wraps the blanket back around her body, after which he wraps two heavier blankets brought from inside around her. He makes them snug against her body by means of electrical tape. He gives a soft kiss on her light-colored lips and places a strand of tape over her mouth. He picks her up and carries her toward the oak. As he reaches the base of the tree, he kneels and places her inside a large swollen hollow in the trunk.

MAN: I love you, Angelique.

Her eyes are open like moon craters. She makes an awkward moan, as if trying to speak. A tear forms and sinks down her face as she slowly closes her eyes. He rises and looks up, to speak to the owl on the tree's thickest branch.

MAN (con't): Judge not, Mister Owl. It is of her tears that you all will drink. Because only from death can the living be nourished.

He then turns around toward the house and is startled to see a young girl standing at the top of the porch stairs.

MAN (con't): Lorelei—go back to bed, my little angel. Please.

possession

run,

run those fields of gold until they sour. trip through unripe brownish landscape with short breaths though I will catch you. I will pick you up by the throat and crackle bones so you fold and hum like a broken string, sort of unright and ouched in the black moving air.

there was a girl you had—lorelei—gone beyond droogen punches and gasps. not your fault, no. families move but I can still creep and blush downward drifts. and such blood that pours when she sleeps, when you catch her,

a star—dogs sometimes cruise the road, below glows of old galactic explosion. they hunt, sure thing. but they loiter too and wait for papa to say that people just die. it's the way, and to hunt or to bite throats from despair is what compels them to lunge from here to there, a star that bursts sad and unheard, a reason to accept the cold flow.

I know your face, son. it wants to look down and do things uncommon to worlds known. to run paths craggy and blistered to smack a dog in its face and say it's my turn! to say it's your thing to curve roads and suck life from desolate minds with broken hearts! do it—succumb to devil and join the roll of the earth's spin, dizzy yourself to make sense of it.

lorelei, she lay frozen as pluto. you made sure of that—what a girl thinks she can outrun troubled fingers wanting a squeeze? kiss away those closed eyes, kiss those lips, kiss goodbye the vanilla smell from her mouth. kiss away playgrounds and dolls and lemonade stands

and future.
kiss, kiss.

rip van no, siree

he can't motherfucking sleep
      and the earth will dissolve, become ashes
beneath the melting moon
as minutes push toward the hour of alarm   the minutes tick,
        as they tick, tick

     talk to him lover, as you slumber with mussy hair
smeared eyeliner   soft sleepy laments in the quiet room
rouse   as he stirs next to your naked body
overtop the sheets and your tears   always entering bed alone.

     talk to him lover, as he tosses and wonders
that the universe is god's brain   planets are cells
wormholes are memory detours   humans spiraling
in space   his imagination running.

talk to him lover through dysphoric turns that push his mind from smoky bark
that hangs a man in mississippi to cocks that swim upstream toward shy fish
that wade lone creeks home in the dim morning to rotting flowers on a
grandmother's gravestone.

talk to him lover so he won't reimagine a broken youth where divorce was
instead a long vacation and brother left home to join the peace corps and father
always played backyard catch and mother never valiumed herself in the
bathroom.

     talk to him lover, talk to him before the moon
falls into his eyes   to further penetration of the self   rub
his temples   ease the fraught movements that
maul his waking mind   help him brush the dirt from pine-boxed pining

that causes suffering to his heart
      so he may motherfucking sleep
      and wake a man cleansed of all the nothingness in his own universe.

albert wolfe

Was is what we say when those we love are gone—such as, *Albert Wolfe was a good man.* He was born in the 1920s and rode the rails from east to west to east again through twenty-two states by the time he was sixteen, where he met hobos & hookers & his share of patrolmen while sleeping in boxcars & brothels & municipal parks beneath yesterday's paper as the ink soaked the past into his blood.

He was the type to live off the measureless land of America with no penny in his pockets but purpose in his rich heart—he moved with motivation to see what the new sun brought each blusterous morning in every new town that would become every old town by nightfall.

And I loved him, my grandfather. Because he was a good man that kept his mind in motion with sights & smells & sounds that I can write about but never know. Not the way he knew, or Evelyn knew—she his wife, and my mother's mother, whom he met at twenty-one and married quickly, yet loved slowly. They ambled together for over fifty years.

Love, he was always telling me—*it's something you just have to have. It makes you more alive than anything on this earth.*

And I watched him all my young years as he smoked packs of unfiltered cigarettes he kept in his left t-shirt pocket, as he took me to Roy's on the first Saturday of each month for a buzz cut, as he told me the stories of his wandering days and the wondering moments that brought him to wake each morning that would compel him to move on to the next town, to see what it was all about—he was chasing love.

And he found it in Evelyn. She was his beauty, with darkest hair of silk, gorgeous velvety eyes. She grounded him; she tamed the husky traveler as no town was able to do. She would make him coffee in the morning before leaving for Jeannette Glass, and kiss his forehead in the evening before putting pork chops on the table, and cover him with a multi-colored afghan when he fell asleep on the sofa during Johnny Carson—because she loved that man as much as he loved his journey to find her.

It turned out that your grandmother was the trip. That thought lingered with me years after he said it, lingered when I heard about the rain-soaked turnpike west of Atlantic City, lingered when I heard of the overturned semi carrying Australian beef—it haunted me when I learned of their minivan crashing into it at sixty miles per hour.

But it comforted me when I learned the sunset dipped with Albert holding her hand, so that they could travel together to spaces the empyreal dark cannot touch for as long as the stars burn in the skies over the measureless land of America, and everywhere.

july 12, 1996

While Awake We Dream
To Break Beyond the Stasis

I was at Ben's, and I tried to explain as best I could the system of existence.

It wasn't an easy moment, of course, being more stoned than a Christian martyr. But it was a try, really. I focused on the presence of people, on the paths of serendipitous meetings and greetings, on how the earth spins to bring poles together. And on chocolate.

ME: Hey—do you ever think about fate?
BEN (shaking head): Nah. Not so much.
ME: Dude. So, take this chocolate, for instance. This perfect and sweet and brilliant box of chocolate. Last week I was at the library, to pick up some Bukowski because this girl I was crushing on is into him. And I really wanted to be into her, right? And wouldn't you know it, there were schoolgirls selling chocolate out front. I bought a box, and I got some Bukowski. After getting home and reading a bit of Bukowski, I put down Bukowski and called the girl immediately and said I wanted nothing to do with her ever. Then I opened the chocolate and ate it. I ate it all, man. So I went back to the library the next day, returned the Bukowski, and I bought two more boxes of chocolate from the same schoolgirls. And while there, in the box-of-chocolate line, I saw a woman so incredibly stunning, I realized I never would have been in that line at that moment if I hadn't hated Bukowski with all my fibers, who I only read because I dug a different girl.

I then converged on the circle of him and Lorelei and me.

ME (con't): Seriously, though—think about it. We are all on our own line. We are on a plane that extends forward and backward: the Future, and the Past. It's always straight. But not everyone's line goes north and south, right? Some lines, though always straight, may be diagonal. And those diagonals enable people to cross the lines of other people at separate times. We are a bunch of lines shooting in all different directions, man. We cross each other at different points. Take you and Lorelei and me for example.

I wrote the following on a piece of paper to visualize things for him:

You   Me   Lorelei

ME (con't): You see? We met first. Then you and Lorelei. Then me and Lorelei.

BEN: You still talk to her?

ME: You know, every so often we bump into each other. I wonder if it was meant to be that way. Like, did I meet her only because I knew you? Or, is it because we were supposed to meet regardless?

BEN: I don't know. I always felt like things just happen. We live, and then we die. And that's it. Nothingness. The Big Sleep.

ME: But—I just can't believe in nothingness. Coincidence, or karma or kismet or fate or happenstance, or pre-destiny, or what-the-fuck ever. People die every day, and we sit back and accept it as the end. No one can prove there's more *beyond* death. It's our perception through observation based on an experience we can't physically experience for ourselves. But what if our line extends onward after we die? Or more specifically, upward—that our line rises like Icarus, untethered to the earth, to disappear into the sun!

BEN: I really wish I was helpful and offered more than this one vital question: can I please have more of that chocolate?

ME: Oh, absolutely. And you know why? Because the only constant currently rambling through the perplexities of my brain is that this here chocolate is sacrament. And I thank my lucky stars I was in line to find it.

And that was that. We smoked more weed in ponderous quiescence, and then we slept. We pushed ourselves into a different realm while coming down from the one we knew, the living place of activity, and conversation, and doubt, and frustration, and complete sadness.

And I very much hated waking each morning knowing that I was always one step farther down my line than I was the day before.

While Asleep We Dream
To Reconcile the Murmurs

I'm sitting on a twin-sized bed centered against the eastern wall in a drab upstairs studio apartment. The room is full of charcoal sketches of a woman that clutter the wooden floor that can only be seen in the moonlight shining through a large window on the southern wall.

Now I see Lorelei, sitting in a meadow naked / cold / shivering. Her back is resting against an enormous solitary oak tree as the sky spins all around her.

Now I'm back in my studio apartment. I look down at the charcoal sketches and wonder why none of them resemble the others quite exactly. There are slight imperfections that would make the observer wonder if they are supposed to be the same woman. I cough a bit and reach for two small white pills on the nightstand. I swallow them with a glass of water and shut my eyes until I begin to feel incredible warmth streaming along my skin. My eyelids become brighter and a breeze messes with my hair.

Now I am sitting on a beach. The sand beneath me is fine / cool / perfect. The expanse off the shore cups the reddish sun as the ocean's crystal waters billow in certain beauty, a dance of liquid and reflection. And I see near identical images of Lorelei enter from the left, arm in arm. They angle toward the water / wade into it / disappear below. Then a giant mermaid emerges as the sun becomes an eclipse in the sky.

Now I am back in the studio apartment. Frenzied, I rise from the bed and walk to an empty canvas queued on an easel in the exact center of the room. I pick up a piece of charcoal and begin to sketch. I draw in the darkness fast and faster and most feverishly!

It's a quick exercise. It must be perfect, I think. I crawl back onto the bed and close my eyes.

Soon the sun breaks through the window and crushes the dark room. I hear cars on the busy street below / the sounds of busy birds tweeting in the morning sky / the moans of busy lovers next door through the wall. They all make a sweet resound through the empty apartment as I snap open my curious eyes. I look over to the picture on the canvas. But it looks bare. I rub my eyes / refocus and look once more—nothing.

I exit the bed and walk to the canvas.

It's blank. How, I wonder. I bow my head and notice bits of charcoal all around my feet. I draw her again / again / again / she never comes out the same. I must always draw twice: I draw two versions of the same image for the canvas to hold her.

Why can't I ever get it right?

disappear into the sun

— an epilogue

This is a strange thing.

VOICE: Welcome—are you quite okay?
ME: No.
VOICE: This will pass. You are experiencing what we call *Decompression.*
ME: I'm very hot.
VOICE: That's understandable. We're in the middle of the Sun.
ME: Oh.
VOICE: Just remain still. You will slowly begin to feel your senses soon enough. Then we can chat a bit about why you're here.
ME: Thank you. I'll—I'll just float here, I guess. And, why is it I'm *floating,* exactly?
VOICE: Well, the Sun isn't a solid mass. So—there really isn't much else to do but float.
ME: I see. That makes sense. But—and I'm really sorry for all these questions—but, why is it that I'm in the middle of the Sun?
VOICE: It's because your line reached upward. And you're dead.
ME: I'm?—Oh. I see.
VOICE: I'm going to ask you a series of questions. This will help me to better assess your situation.
ME: My situation?
VOICE: This should all make more sense soon enough. May I begin?
ME: Please do.
VOICE: Thank you. What is your entire name?
ME: C. Aloysius Mariotti—Chris.
VOICE: Where were you born?
ME: I believe it was in the belly of a thorn bush.
VOICE: I see. And, what is your first childhood memory?
ME: I—don't know. All I can see are myriad images, like snapshots or postcards, right? But I can't seem to separate them by date. Is that odd?
VOICE: Not at all, Mister Chris. During *Decompression,* the mind is aflutter with scattered memories. This process helps to get them back in order.
ME: Okay.
VOICE: I'm going to continue—have you ever committed a sin?
ME: It depends. I've done some deplorable things, sure. But—wait. Who are you?
VOICE: I'm the Limbo Man, Mister Chris. You can call me Icarus.
ME: Icarus? As in wax wings, flew too close to the sun?
ICARUS: The very one, yes.

ME: Strange.

ICARUS: Not really. We all have our lot, and this is mine.

ME: But you are a myth.

ICARUS: So are you, to some people. But we're digressing. Please—continue regarding the *deplorable things* you mentioned.

ME: Well—I suppose sin is a subjective word. But—yes. I've committed a few.

ICARUS: And, were these acts done of selfishness or necessity? In your opinion, please.

ME: Maybe a little of both—depending on the circumstance.

ICARUS: Do you feel justified in your participation of such deplorable acts regardless of the circumstance? Or, perhaps more to the heart of it—would you do the very same things again?

ME: May I interrupt momentarily?

ICARUS: Well, we are on a bit of a roll though.

ME: I know. And I apologize. But, I need to ask you something, and your answer may help me better answer your question.

ICARUS: Then of course. What is it, Mister Chris?

ME: Why did you fly too close to the Sun? Because the stories of you aren't overly flattering concerning your hubris, or common sense, you see? And you seem like a bright and centered and polite fellow. I just wonder if there's something behind the perception.

ICARUS: In fact, there is. There are such things as ghosts, Mister Chris. But they aren't physical creatures that toil and haunt with chains and moans. They are only the memories of people not quite forgotten. They linger in stories. I am a ghost. I am the memory of me. I am *your* memory of me.

ME: So—well, I'm not sure I understand.

ICARUS: Everyone dies, Mister Chris. And there is an afterlife. But this is the place everyone goes first.

ME: The Sun?

ICARUS: Well—no. Limbo. It's the phase immediately following physical death.

ME: Why is this place *my* Limbo?

ICARUS: Because you believed completely in the act of rising up, of straying from the straight line, of reaching the Sun. Let me ask—do you feel as though there is one true religion?

ME: I don't know. Honestly, I could never commit to a single belief behind any concept of religion. Thomas Paine once said, "My own mind is my own church." And I took that to heart very much.

ICARUS: Is it because you didn't need a physical structure, or organization, to speak to God?

ME: Yes.

ICARUS: So more than religion, you believed in a certain spirituality?

45

ME: I guess I believed in a chance for the individual to attain a higher consciousness. It seems like most religions, or beliefs, share very similar traits. They only differ in particulars. In that sense, I always thought they were all basically the same.

ICARUS: But you never attached yourself to one?

ME: No. *My own mind is my own church.* Nature is God. And life on Earth is a chance to gain experience, to attempt reaching that higher consciousness.

ICARUS: So it wouldn't surprise you that a Christian would be talking to Saint Peter right now instead of me?

ME: I guess it makes sense if that's what the individual believed in.

ICARUS: And you believed in rising above the straight line, in reaching the Sun. You see, the Limbo Man is the same Man to everyone. He just has a different face to the Dead.

ME: And you're my face.

ICARUS: Yes—I am the symbol of attempting to rise above my own straight line, which was your personal philosophy of attaining that higher consciousness of which you speak.

ME: I see. And what about an Atheist? Who does he see?

ICARUS: He sees himself. And he battles to understand the knowledge that he isn't simply rotting in the ground. And when he understands, he returns to the earth to seek out the concept of a higher consciousness post-mortem.

ME: Reincarnation?

ICARUS: Of course. Humans cannot reach that higher consciousness without wanting to. The cycle resumes, over and over, until the image of its possibility is realized. Hindus, for example, never believe they have lived their best life. That's why reincarnation is such a strong component of their religion. They try to shed their imperfections on earth to ultimately become one with the Divine Source.

ME: And what's Heaven for Christians?

ICARUS: That concept is built around faith that it exists. But, Heaven isn't merely a vast field of lovely grass with winged seraphs greeting the Christian. Heaven is the Hindu reuniting with the Source. Heaven is the reversal of the Atheist's methodology of an afterlife. Heaven is the place just beyond your Sun. Heaven is higher consciousness, Mister Chris. They are all the same but pronounced differently.

ME: Okay—so, right now I'm speaking to you to examine if I'm ready to attain higher consciousness?

ICARUS: Precisely. That's *Decompression.* My questions help determine whether you have relieved yourself of all that is necessary for you to accomplish the move from earth to beyond.

ME: And what is your current prognosis?

ICARUS: I need you to return to my last question—would you do the very same things again?

ME: No—I don't think I would.

ICARUS: What would you change?

ME: Well, I'm redeemed in how everything turned out to an extent. But, I think I could've made decisions early on that would've had me avoid those certain eventual deplorable things.

ICARUS: Such as?

ME: I think if I could've been a stronger person, if I could've helped Lorelei when she needed me, it would've aimed me toward many different decisions. Better decisions.

ICARUS: It stems back to Lorelei?

ME: I believe so, yes. I think if I could've helped her, many lives would have been affected more positively. Might, might, might. But, I believe this to be true.

ICARUS: *Decompression* is now complete, Mister Chris.

ME: And?

ICARUS: And—I need to send you back. Because of your admittance to a personal failure, you are unable to forge ahead currently. Until you right what you believe was a wrong, you cannot logically be eligible for higher consciousness.

ME: What happens now?

ICARUS: You get your chance to make amends with the source of your regret. You will be reincarnated with the hope that you can make a difference to the person you believe you failed.

ME: Lorelei—how?

ICARUS: Did you know that Lorelei was pregnant at the time of your death?

ME: Jesus—what?

ICARUS: Her son. It is you. And with this opportunity, I hope you can mend the failures for which you believe you are responsible. Before you go, Mister Chris, I need to inform you that your sensibilities will always exist. You will always reach for the Sun—you always have, each time we've met. And with good fortune, the next time we meet, you will be absolved of this burden. The next time we meet, sir, I hope you will be confident and prepared to attain the higher consciousness you have always sought throughout the centuries— Godspeed, Mister Chris.

Acknowledgements

Thank you to the following for first publishing the poems included in this book, often in different versions:

Black Bough Poetry: "desert diptych" (first published as two separate poems);
Boston Accent Lit: "impeachment day";
Burning House Press: "may 10, 1981";
Dark Marrow: "modern pip, fragmented";
The Failure Baler: "modern adonis";
The Hellebore Press: "lost american gospel of vincent de paul";
Marias at Sampaguitas: "saint de los milagros";
Neon Mariposa Magazine: "possession";
Rhythm & Bones Lit: "albert wolfe" (nominated for a Pushcart Prize).

∞

Massive gratitude to the talented artists who provided the beautiful artwork included inside this book:

Mathew Yates: *pg. 3, 9, 19, 25, 37, 49.*

Stuart Buck: *pg. 34:*

∞

"the pendulum swings a strange loop," "I wondered about love for a moment," and "in vertigo" are excerpts from a larger unpublished manuscript called *Collapse the Light into Earth.*

Gratitude

Thank you to my wife, Kristen, for your boundless love and support since that very first night our unfettered hearts entwined and merged.

Thank you to my mom for always encouraging my curiosity, my strangeness, and my love for the Beatles; to my father for teaching me about redemption and forgiveness.

To Mathew Yates, your art throughout this book elevates the words to heights beyond the stars and moon. To Stuart Buck, your owl and tree art is perfect serendipity.

To my writing family, The Legend City Collective: Holly Pelesky, Tianna G. Hansen, Kari A. Flickinger, Stuart Buck, Carla Sofia Ferreira, Nadia Gerassimenko, Paul Rowe, Kiley Lee, Marisa Silva-Dunbar, and Danielle Rose. Your indelible brilliance and love pushes me to be better in my craft and my life.

To the following individuals for their friendship, support, and inspiration: Jeff Victorian, Daniel Mariotti, Simon Kennedy, Carrie Eden, Jeff Fay, Karly DiBella, Jason Collins, Rueben Rodriguez, K.B. Carle, Kristi Weber, Ankh Spice, and Chip McCabe.

Thank you to everyone who read the book in advance to offer a review, feedback, and advice.

Thank you to Rhythm & Bones Press and Tianna G. Hansen for giving this book a life outside my own mind. My gratitude spreads with every moment because of your faith and trust in me and my words.

Thank you to everyone who's read, shared, and published my work. None of this would've happened without you.

And to my darling Westie, Bella Francine Mariotti. Just for being.

About the Author

C. Aloysius Mariotti was born in Pennsylvania and raised in Arizona. He studied creative writing at the University of Arizona, where he listened to a lot of Rush, Radiohead, and PJ Harvey. His work has been featured in Black Bough Poetry, The Hellebore, Marias at Sampaguitas, Memoir Mixtapes, and Dark Marrow, among others. He resides in Massachusetts with his wife Kristen and Westie Bella Francine.

SCREAM into my MOUTH as a WATERFALL is his first collection.

∞

About the Artists

Mathew Yates is a disabled, queer artist & poet from Kentucky. Their work can be found in Barren Magazine, Kissing Dynamite Poetry, Epigraph Magazine, Memoir Mixtapes, and more. When not being an agoraphobic hermit, Mathew enjoys being a reclusive cavefish. Variety is the spice of life.

Stuart Buck is a visual artist and award-winning poet living in North Wales. His art has been featured in several journals, as well as gracing the covers of several books. His third poetry collection, *Portrait of a Man on Fire*, is forthcoming from Rhythm & Bones Press in November 2020. He is the art editor for Kanstellation Magazine and available for commissions all year round. Find more at stuartbuck.co.uk.

About the Press

Rhythm & Bones Press is a small independent press founded by Tianna G. Hansen, dedicated to dynamic and inspiring authors whose work deserves to be shared and acknowledged. They specialize in authors who write with personal emotion and those with trauma to portray to the world. They help turn Trauma into Art. Be sure to check out this book on GoodReads and leave a review, and follow them on Twitter @RhythmBonesLit, Instagram or Facebook @RhythmBonesPress. Find more of their books at rhythmnbone.com/books.

∞

Coming Soon

Violence/Joy/Chaos
April 2020

Leaving Arizona
May 2020

Voices for the Cure:
An Anthology by People with ALS and their Caregivers
June 2020

A View from the Phantasmagoria
October 2020

Portrait of a Man on Fire
November 2020

CPSIA information can be obtained
at www.ICGtesting.com
Printed in the USA
BVHW092024080320
574285BV00001B/3